Grace will walk us home

A daily discipline of Bible readings and short prayers

Grace will walk us home

A daily discipline of Bible readings and short prayers

Thom M Shuman

wild goose
publications

www.ionabooks.com

Overseas distribution
Australia: Willow Connection Pty Ltd, Unit 4A, 3–9 Kenneth Road, Manly
Vale, NSW 2093
New Zealand: Pleroma, Higginson Street, Otane 4170, Central Hawkes Bay
Canada: Bayard Distribution, 10 Lower Spadina Ave., Suite 400, Toronto,
Ontario M5V 2Z

Printed by Bell & Bain, Thornliebank, Glasgow

Introduction

In 30+ years of ministry, I have taught studies on just about every book in the Bible. As a preacher, I've gone through the 3-year cycle of Sunday readings over 9 times. So, I have spent a lot of 'professional' time in the Bible. But I had never really read through the Bible from beginning to end to feed my own spiritual life, until recently. I used one of those structured programmes that allows one to read several chapters (an Old and New Testament reading), and either a Psalm or a reading from Proverbs, each day. I used it not only for the discipline of Bible reading, but also to enhance my daily practice of writing. I would discover a word, a phrase, a verse or two which spoke to me, let it play around in my mind and heart for a while, and then write a brief nudge. At the end of the year, I had 365 of them (plus one for a leap year), which are shared with you in these pages. I hope they speak to your heart and soul in some way.

Thom M Shuman

Day 1

Genesis 2:2

and on the eighth day,
you said:
share the light;
give everyone a cool drink;
feed those around you;
dance under the stars;
explore the skies and waters;
be gentle with every creature;
you are not alone …
… and relax (it's not all about you).

Day 2

Genesis 4:6–7

stuffing our arms
into anger's sleeves
and yanking up bitterness'
zipper, we
stomp out of the
house,
slamming the door
behind us, never noticing
Short Coming nipping
at our heels, until
we trip and fall
flat
on our souls.

Day 3

Matthew 3:11

you come,
kneeling down to
untie our foolishness
from around our souls so,
barefoot,
we may run through
the sprinklers with you,
until we are swept
up
in Spirit's arms.

Day 4

Genesis 9:16

at the end
of the curved colours,
we hope to
find a wee man with
a pot of gold
just for us, and
so miss the
heart overflowing
with grace, hope and
love,
just for us.

Day 5

Matthew 5:16

sadly,
we have become
nightlights of
comfort so the
quo can sleep
without waking,
rather
than beacons of hope
for those suffering
from injustice,
hatred and
no status.

Day 6

Matthew 5:42

we have heard
you
say we are to
help others (but
only
if they can jump
through certain
hoops
devised
by those who
have no need

for anything
because we have
so much of everything,
correct?)

Day 7

Matthew 6:16

but
if no one
sees how miserable
i am while
following you, how
will they know
how much you
mean to
me?

Day 8

Genesis 18:1–2

may we be
as eager to
embrace the strangers
you send to us, as
we are in welcoming
our best friends
into our hearts.

Day 9

Matthew 8:1–2

instead of turning
our backs,
we could be the
hope,
healing,
forgiveness,
grace
others need in their lives,
if we choose.

Day 10

Genesis 21:9–10

forgive us when
we, who are so
graced by you,
show such bad
manners towards
those around us
who are struggling,
different,
a seeming threat.

Day 11

Matthew 9:21

with a hat and gloves,
we can warm
the rough sleeper;
with a smile,
we can ease
the child's fears;
with a word,
we can cradle
the senior's loneliness;
and bring healing
to our selfish
apathy.

Day 12

Matthew 10:31

perhaps
the most vulnerable
in our midst
would be less fearful
of us, if
we offered them
the same love,
compassion,
care
we shower on our
dogs, cats, pet birds.

Day 13

Matthew 11:4

when we see immigrants
welcomed with joy
or
injustice brought
to its knees;
when we listen to
children speak out
against bullies
or
rough sleepers invite
others to share a meal,
how
can we not run
to share this good news?

Day 14

Matthew 11:16

the generation which
balkanises the playground
so everyone knows
their place and
never crosses the line,
or the one which
welcomes and teaches

games from outsiders
and learns new ones
from them …

which shall we be?

Day 15

Psalm 9:13a

Lord, be gracious
to those who have suffered
from my hurtful words,
my cavalier arrogance,
my thoughtless disdain,
my (dare I admit) hate;
especially when i could have
lifted them up with
grace
comfort
hope
love
instead.

Day 16

Proverbs 2:9

when we hunger
to do the harder right
rather than the easier
expediency;
when our thirst
for justice will
not be quenched by
sugary platitudes;
when fairness breaks out
in the corridors of
power and
not just on
playgrounds,
we will have found your way.

Day 17

Psalm 10:1–2

when we could stand
next to others,
holding their hearts,
why do we edge
away from the bullied?
When we could confront
those who would take away
services to the poor,

why do we hide behind
our walls of
good intentions?

kyrie eleison.

Day 18

Genesis 37:24

they come with
dreams cradled in their
hopes:
that children can be lifted
out of poverty;
that peace could emerge
from the ashes of war;
that people just might
learn how to love each other,
and
we toss them and their dreams
in the empty bin, as
we watch reality shows
hosted by con artists
eager to fill our hollow souls
with even more emptiness.

Day 19

Matthew 13:44

we could mend
crumbling and
hungering-for-hope
neighbourhoods,
but since we think
no one of value resides
in such places, we
spend the money
on ourselves
(again).

Day 20

Matthew 14:14

when
we step over
the homeless on our way
to buy another
$5 coffee;
we give our
castoffs to the
shivering kids instead
of a new coat;
we throw out
enough food to
feed another
family,

we have left our
compassion
back in the boat
once again.

Day 21

Matthew 14:31

when we wonder
if the new captain even
knows the bow
from the stern;
when we worry
that justice
will be jettisoned
over the side;
when we fear
that the vulnerable
will be left behind,
may the winds of faith
continue to refresh us,
so we may journey
with you until we reach
the shores of compassion,
inclusion,
peace and
hope.

Day 22

Genesis 43:30

noticing the scarfed
teenager sitting alone
on the bus;
listening to the
immigrant child
translating for his
parents;
comforting those
who find themselves
outsiders looking in,
we meet our family,
and weep
for our loss in
not knowing them
all our lives.

Day 23

Psalm 14:6

we hold hoops
for the poor
to jump through,
while you make
snow angels with them;
we write regulations

enabling the hungry
to receive our leftovers,
while you take them
out for dinner;
we look down our noses
at those standing on corners
with hand-scrawled appeals,
and you offer them
a lift to your heart.

Day 24

Proverbs 3:3

from the jewellery box
on top of the bureau,
you take the necklace
crafted long ago by Spirit
when she was young,
with beads of hope strung
on the strands of kinship,
and placing it
around our neck, you
whisper, 'you'll
always have my heart.'

Day 25

Psalm 15:1–2

except for those
detours down
apathy's alley,
surely our footsteps
are firm;
apart from wanting
things done our way
(only on the rarest
of occasions!),
surely we are
on the side of righteousness;
other than those
daggers we hurl
from our hearts
at others,
surely we are
people of veracity.

Day 26

Psalm 16:1

may we be
the umbrella
for those
showered by hate;
the cradling lap
for children who

tremble in the night;
the heart hollowed by grief
so we can embrace
all who have lost everything;
even
as you are all
this (and more)
for us.

Day 27

Job 5:16

may hope be
not a long stare
through the poor,
but a welcome
to our tables;
nor a rueful grin
as we mime
empty pockets –
but a bear hug
of joy.
May injustice's tantalising
seductive whispers of
'they must wait their turn'
be silenced by
the singing of 'we
shall overcome'.

Day 28

Matthew 19:21

i hold tight
to all my resources, just
waiting for the right moment,
person,
effort
to share, and
so remain a
saint of indecision,
shuffling my feet
away from
you.

Day 29

Psalm 17:6

when others act
as if they cannot
understand my shouts,
you hear my
sore-throated whispers;
when my friends(!)
turn their hearts
away from me, you
put your ear
right next
to my lips

to cradle every
ache.

Day 30

Job 15:31

when we
gorge ourselves
on pleasant
platitudes,
stuff politicians'
hollow words
down our throats,
imbibe bottle after
bottle of
fragrant whines,
is it any wonder
we feel so
empty
all the time?

Day 31

Matthew 21:10

this is the interpreter
who supported your
children in war zones;
this is the doctor
who could bring

healing to many;
this is the child
longing to run
into her mother's arms;
this is the refugee
who brings nothing
but hope in his heart;

help us to lay down
our turmoiling fears
and welcome them.

Day 32

Job 22:7

when we could
hand the parched
a cup of grace,
we offer them
disappointment's dust;
when we could
prepare a meal for
those who hunger
for acceptance, we
padlock the pantry,
pocketing the key
as we walk
away

have mercy, Lord …

Day 33

Job 28:3–4

may we never forget
those who clean up
after us as we
travel;
the farmers and migrants
in the shadows
before dawn,
harvesting the food
we take for granted;
the electrical lineworkers
who climb poles
in wild winds and bitter cold
so we might keep
warm.

Day 34

Job 31:6

our
stress, fears, foolish
choices, nightmares
are gradually piled on
and we slowly begin
to sink deeper,
then
you place kilo-grace
after kilo-grace in
the weighing pan
until we are tipped
towards your
love.

Day 35

Matthew 23:8

we could put
more letters after
our names,
or teach a
child to read;
we could build
a wall to hold our
awards and diplomas,
or construct a
bridge of hope;

we could sew
bars on our
robes,
or set free
the oppressed;
we could read
more books,
or open our hearts
to you.

Day 36

Proverbs 4:7

in a time of
alt-facts
and news cranked
out by counterfeiters, may
we discover
wisdom
in the weakness
to serve others;
understanding
in the laughter
of children on
a playground;
insight
in the innate
compassion of
the overlooked.

Day 37

Matthew 24:35

when fear threatens
to blow it away,
you whisper, and
hope digs in its heels;
when bitterness would
throw it in a bin,
you sing, and
love is recycled
in little children;
when haters would
have their way,
you protest, and
justice welcomes outsiders
into their new homes.

Day 38

Matthew 25:44

should i
offer a cup of water
to those who parch
the souls of the needy;
set a place
at the table for
all who would build
walls to limit outsiders;

drop off a casserole
to those locked
in fear's cells;
provide a lift to
the doctor's office
for the legislator
who voted against
affordable care for all;
give my coat
to the shivering
pro-life marcher,
or
just keep butting
my head against
my self-righteousness?

Day 39

Exodus 2:16–17

we could sit
by the side
of society, watching
and twittering about
all those who are
shoved aside,
ridiculed,
walled out,
or
we can stand up
to the bullies,

welcoming everyone
to the well of
justice.

Day 40

Proverbs 4:14–15

rather than taking
the expressway
to foolishness, may
your grace-positioning system
turn us down
the back roads
of hope;
instead of slinking down
the cracked pavement
of temptation, may
we play hopscotch
on the sidewalks of
the kingdom.

Day 41

Psalm 19:10a

i could keep
grace,
peace,
hope,
joy
stuffed deep in
my pockets, or
offer them
to everyone who
stands by the side
of life, holding
a heart-drawn sign
reading,
'can you help?'

Day 42

Psalm 20:1–3

may God answer you
with those who long
to learn your name;
with cities, neighbourhoods,
strangers offering you
a safe welcome;
with those who
remember
you are as gifted

as they;
with those who
honour the sacrifices
you have made
on your journey.

Day 43

Matthew 27:23

we take great umbrage
at the seasick little girl
in a refugee boat;
the woman in front
of us using food stamps;
the family struggling
to learn the language
of their new home, but
remain silent whenever
injustice roars,
lies prowl our streets,
hate promotes a seminar,
anger offers a feast.

Lord, have mercy.

Day 44

Matthew 27:54

though it is
no angel of the

Lord,
but an officer
of the empire;
no heavenly host,
but a band of
seasoned, battle-scarred,
cynical conscripts,
the song is the
same
at the finish as it is
at the beginning of
the story:
God is here!

Day 45

Matthew 28:1

on the second day,
we could
teach magic tricks
to a bunch of
wide-eyed kids;
sing love songs
to the residents
in a memory unit;
give a lift
to the travellers
by the side of
society, or
just put our feet up
and relax, as if

the stone has been
rolled back to
silence the
good news.

Day 46

Psalm 22:2

in the little girl
at the bus stop
who smiles, 'hello!';
in the barista
who hands us a
cuppa, winking,
'it's on the house';
in the neighbour
who knocks on
the door after
dinner, offering,
'how about a piece
of cake?';
in the grandchild
falling asleep in
our arms, singing,
'i love you'

you speak,
but
are we listening?

Day 47

Exodus 19:8a

of course,
we will do
everything
you ask of us!

except for
welcoming the outsider,
lifting up the fallen,
caring for the most vulnerable,
loving our enemies,
forgiving over and over,
sharing from our abundance,
and other ridiculous ideas
we know you haven't
really thought through.

Day 48

Exodus 22:26–27

compassion:

the coat gathering
dust in the closet,
warming a refugee;
the staples sitting
on the pantry shelf,
feeding folk at a shelter;

the arm which could
push away the bullied teenager,
reaching out to draw
him into comfort;
the ear tuned to the
latest reality show,
listening to the
grief of a widow.

Day 49

Mark 4:26–27

the further we
are willing to
journey with
faith,
holding fast to
her hands, sharing
each meal, and
a sleeping bag
at night, the
closer we come
to that place
which awaits
us.

Day 50

Psalm 23:5a

in the midst of
those who trouble
us, may
we lay out a
picnic,
so, in the breaking
of the bread,
hearts might be
mended,
old slights brushed
away with the
crumbs,
and bridges built
across the blanket
spread over grace's
lawn.

Day 51

Psalm 24:6

in the little kids
who read to
the cats and dogs
at the no-kill shelter;
in the teenagers
gathering up blankets
for those who

sleep on the streets;
in the retirees
who travel the country
as Mr and Mrs Claus
to visit children in hospitals;
in all who do more
unnoticed
than all the attention-
seekers ever accomplish,
we discover the
company
we should keep.

Day 52

Mark 6:8

with

your love
which can overcome
hate;
your hope
which can fill
despair's emptiness;
your grace
which can change
all lives (even
ours);
your peace
which can build
bridges to others,

we have all we
need
to go out into the world
every day.

Day 53

Exodus 32:3–4

taking the
shouts of anger,
alternative facts of
fear,
whispers of woe
from our ears, we
melt them down
into those gods
we would rather
worship than
you.

Day 54

Psalm 25:9

when we long
for that ticker-tape
parade,
riding through the
self-congratulatory
confetti
showered on us

for all we have,
set us on
that cracked sidewalk
so we can follow
you
to serve those
who need everything.

Day 55

Mark 8:2

on the third
day,
roll way the stone
from the tomb
where we have
interred our
compassion,
so it may be
resurrected
to offer hope
to those around
us.

Day 56

Mark 8:21

when we think
the leftover pieces

of hope are not
worth saving,
when we step
over the homeless
on our way
to the seminar
on discipleship,
when we spend more time
on retweeting and reposting
than on working to restore
justice to those around us,
we show we still
don't have a clue
about the kingdom.

Day 57

Mark 9:10

we spend so
much time
theologising,
analysing,
seminarising
this rising conundrum,
that folk looking for
hope,
life,
grace and
joy
turn somewhere
else.

Day 58

Mark 9:34

in our social
media uproar over
the latest awards
fiasco,
the foolish words
of vain people,
the lyrics of the platinumest
singer around, our
silence
concerning the most
vulnerable
in our midst is
deafening.

Day 59

Psalm 27:10

when folk padlock
their hearts so
i can't get in;
when the world
packs my belongings,
leaving the suitcase
out on the front
porch for when i
arrive home from
life;

when friends
continually change
their mobile #s,
so i can't
reach them,
you
gather me
in your arms,
enveloping me
in grace.

Day 60

Proverbs 6:18

we hope
you will replace the
grudge-positioning system
lodged in our
hearts, which
recalculates us until
we turn down
the wrong roads,
with your grace
so
we can finally
find our way
back to you.

Day 61

Psalm 28:1

just a
word:
of grace,
or hope,
maybe love
or even
reprimand,
can keep me
from
falling into that
mess
where I can
never find my
way out (on
my own).

Day 62

Mark 11:27

however
many times it takes,
you will
continue to
come into our
fears, our
worries, our
resistance, until

we finally see
you for who you
are:
the One
we need
again and
again.

Day 63

Mark 12:15b

as long as
we
keep putting
you
to the test,
we
can keep failing
you,
and not have
to answer any
of
your
(more difficult)
questions.

Day 64

Proverbs 6:22

with each step, may
i place my foot
in the imprint left
by compassion
following it to care
for others;
in the silent hours of
the night, may
i curl up
in hope's
lap;
in the morning, may
wonder and joy
leap into my bed
yelling, 'get up,
sleepyhead! it's a new
day!'

Day 65

Mark 13:23

we keep wanting
to leap ahead
in the story to
find out how it
will end, forgetting

that the final Word
was written
long before
'in the beginning'
was penned.

Day 66

Mark 14:16

if we only trusted,
we could find your
promised gifts
to enable us
to turn rusted-out
factories into
training programmes;
to transform empty
shopping malls into
hospitals;
to reimagine closed
schools as
memory care centres;
and we could lead
folk (including us)
out of their bondage of
despair.

Day 67

Mark 14:27a

when we
maroon
folk on poverty's isle;
when we
play hooky
from learning
the hopes of little children;
when we
run away
rather than racing
to lift up those
cast aside by power;
when we
slack off
from the simple
task of faithfulness,
you shake your
head (but
still keep offering
another chance).

Day 68

Leviticus 19:9–10

when we stock
more food than
we will ever
eat

before it goes bad,
rather than sharing
with the hungry,
we glean what little
hope
remains for others,
leaving their hearts as
empty
as their stomachs.

Day 69

Psalm 31:19a

the flower peeking
through the snow;
the warm sun
swimming across
the clear sky;
the gentle breezes
which scatter leaves;
friends who love us
no matter, and
strangers who smile
unexpectedly,
yet

we grumble at
our
empty
lives.

Day 70

Psalm 32:9

when i snort
with impatience,
stomping my feet
and banging around
the stall of your
heart,
rest your hand
upon me, calming
my spirit with
the taste of your
grace, gentling
me with hope's
caress.

Day 71

Leviticus 25:35

if the family from
Aleppo
are my cousins;
if the immigrant
mum
working 3 jobs
is my sister;
if the Muslim
teenager
is my son;

if the hungry
girl
is my daughter,
how
can i turn
my back on
any
(or all)
of them?

Day 72

Proverbs 7:4

like the sister
who always listens
to the deep echoes
of our hearts;
like the *anam cara*
who hears the
whispers of our
souls even
before we do,
Spirit
shadows our every
step,
moment,
breath.

Day 73

Psalm 33:12

happy is God, when
we do not make
the Lord
a political idol, but
offer mercy
to all in
need
(without requiring
multiple IDs and
proof of misery),
establish justice
wherever oppression
would build
barriers,
welcome the gifts
offered to us by
the very ones
we are taught
are not
family.

Day 74

Psalm 34:8a

in the kneading
of the cat
alarm each morning;
in the sticky-fingered
grip of the
preschoolers;
in the sloppy
kiss of the
neighbour's dog;
in the glass of
cold milk chasing
down the warm pie;
in the gentle breath
of love on
the pillow next to
me,
i discover your
sweet goodness
and am
filled.

Day 75

Psalm 34:14

we train for
months
for malice's
marathon, but
can never seem
to find the
stamina
to cross the
street to offer
peace
to the
exhausted.

Day 76

Luke 2:20

we could
be listening
to the good news
sung
by the most
ignored
among us, but
we drown out their
joy,
grumbling,
'why aren't they
back on the hillside

where they
belong?'

Day 77

Psalm 35:10

when the rich
assume the poor
have everything
they could ever
need,
you clean out
all your theology books
from the cluttered den
to turn it into
a guest room;
when the politicians
cut funding for
meals to those
who truly
hunger, as
they head off
to their reserved
tables at
Chez Arrogance,
you head to
the kitchen, prepping
and cooking meals
to serve to your
neighbours.

Day 78

Psalm 35:13–14

we could
actually
care for the
grieving,
the sick,
the broken, by
staying by their sides,
cradling their tears,
mending their hearts,
but it is usually
easier
to shed crocodile
tears and
offer pious platitudes.

Day 79

Luke 3:10–11

as we take
the coats
that have waited
for months in our
closets to be used,
and put them around
the weatherworn;
as we take
the food from

our shelves that
we bought for
that recipe we
lost so long ago,
and bring it
to the food bank,
may we open
our hearts to
the hope
you
never hesitate to
share.

Day 80

Numbers 11:23

we continue to believe
evil is
inexhaustible,
fear knows
no boundaries,
anger never
runs out of excuses,
hate is
infinite, but
are convinced
you
have cut back
your hours to
part-time.

Day 81

Luke 4:37

too often, the
report about you
reaches
every region of
our soul
and
lies there
gathering dust
while we
twitter on
about
inanities.

Day 82

Psalm 37:1

when we see
the frightening images
of attacks on innocents,
of apartments on fire,
may we remember
the strangers
kneeling to comfort
an unknown sister,
the responders
leaving their fear

behind as they run
to help;
people
refusing the easy
choice to
not care.

Day 83

Psalm 37:16

instead of
waiting for
the lottery winnings
(or pot of gold)
to magically
appear,
remind us that
whatever
we have is
enough
to help those
who have been
waiting for
hope.

Day 84

Numbers 20:13

we would rather
jump feet first
into quibble's
deep waters, sinking
down
to grab
contention's bones
lying on the
bottom,
than take the
glass
of peace
you hold out to
us.

Day 85

Psalm 37:24

when we tumble off
faith's seat,
you bandage
our skinned knees,
tighten the
training wheels and
adjust the seat
so our legs can

reach hope and
grace, as
we learn to ride
the sidewalks
of your kingdom.

Day 86

Luke 6:49a

if i don't translate
your words into
a home for
refugees,
a meal for
the hungry,
a book for
a child,
a bottle of medicine for
the sick,
have i truly
been
listening?

Day 87

Luke 7:20

while we drum
our fingers on
our faded dreams
waiting for the
one who will restore
our might,
our greatness,
our wealth,
our membership,
you
are rescuing the
immigrants,
giving medicine
to the sick,
picking up those
who have stumbled,
opening the eyes
of the unwilling,
and waiting
for us to stop asking
and start doing.

Day 88

Proverbs 8:14

i could sign up
for another seminar, or
learn football from

the kids in the street;
i could put up
more shelves for
more books, or
listen to the stories of
my neighbours;
i could earn
another degree, or
learn a new language
from a co-worker;
i could remain
a know-it-all,
or start from scratch
with you.

Day 89

Psalm 38:15

when i rush
about, be
my yield
sign;
when i spin
in giddy
circles, be
my *caim*;
when i tap my
feet impatiently, be
a waltz;
when i babble
a hundred words

a second, be
silence's
soft whisper, so
i may discover
you in the
patience.

Day 90

Psalm 39:12

whether our hearts
can only whisper
or
we are swearing
at the top of our
lungs,
you listen;
whether we are
dressed for the prom
or
wearing our
faded hand-me-downs,
you welcome us;
whether we can
pull out a
multi-page genealogy
report
or
have just arrived,
we are your
children.

Day 91

Psalm 40:4

the arrogant bait
their hooks with
enticing morsels
of power, hoping
to hook us and
carry us home
to mount on their
walls, so
help us drift
along on the
living waters, content
to be lazy with
you.

Day 92

Proverbs 8:30

if we would
only stop
trying to be
so adult in
order to get
you to approve
of us,
we might discover
you love us
simply

because we are
your
children.

Day 93

Psalm 40:13

not an obligation
nor something
to cross off your
to-do list, but
you reclaim us
because
it completes your heart;
not shutting the
window
so you won't hear,
nor reluctant to
get out of your
chair,
you rush out
the door to assist
us whenever
we call.

Day 94

Deuteronomy 1:31–32

because
the photos are

faded and curled,
the stories are
dismissed as fanciful
and
the tellers are
seen as ancient, we
remain unconvinced
about cradling the
cares of others,
and leave them
behind in their

desolations.

Day 95

Deuteronomy 4:9

we can show
our kids and
grandkids
pictures of all
the wrong others
do, or
let them watch
the videos of
the helpers and
repairers;

we can let goodness
slip through the
crevices of our

brains into
nothingness, or
hand it on
to those walking
after us.

Day 96

Proverbs 8:34

i could sit
on the porch
steps,
eager for Foolishness
to finish breakfast and
come out to
play tag, or
i could curl
up in your lap,
as you read
me stories of
hope
and
grace.

Day 97

Luke 11:33

when we would
box you up
and store you

in the basement
with the tree, lights
and ornaments, may
we learn to sit
with you at the
living room window,
your soul glowing as
you wait for
the prodigals to
come home.

Day 98

Deuteronomy 10:19

we could
change the code
on the security system
every 12 hours,
install steel-plated
doors front and back,
put guard dogs out
in the yard
when dusk falls,
or
welcome you
in the immigrants
longing to share
your hope
with us.

Day 99

Deuteronomy 11:2

we could hope
our kids
will figure everything
out, or we
can see your strength
in the little ones
standing up to bullies,
feel your power
in the mothers
protesting injustice,
know your hope
in the arms
that cradle the
patients receiving chemo.

Day 100

Luke 13:18

the kingdom is like
a kitten stalking
a sunbeam, until
it captures it
to share a nap;
a classroom of kids
donating their favourite
books
to a refugee shelter;

a woman passing on
her nana's handwritten
cookie recipes
to her
grandson.

Day 101

Deuteronomy 16:20

i spend months
training, increasing
my miles, focusing
on the upcoming marathon;
i go twice a week
to the boot camp
to get back to
my college weight
and find energy for
the reunion;
i continue to play
sports my doctor
reminds me only
damage my body
more ...

but chasing
justice?

i barely break
a
sweat.

Day 102

Luke 14:27

perhaps
that cross
is simply
the secrets
another confides
in us;
the little child
hoping for someone
to help with
the hard words;
the loneliness
of a neighbour
wandering the
wilderness of
adolescence;
the memories of
a senior citizen
who lives them
over and over
again.

Day 103

Luke 15:13

we've gone to
that far country
called foolishness:
spending grace

on greedy goods;
confusing lust
with love;
mortgaging our hopes
for a place
where our hungers
are filled, wondering
all the while
if you have even
noticed
we are gone.

Day 104

Luke 16:15

when we drop
off groceries at
the pantry, but don't
speak to those waiting
at the door;
when we serve
at the shelter, but
know none of
the guests by name;
when we sing songs
for the residents
at the nursing home,
but don't bother
to listen to their
lives, we
have simply stuck

in our thumb
and pulled out
aplomb,
saying, 'what good
people we are!'

Day 105

Luke 17:5

we keep waiting
for
the lottery numbers
to hit;
the winning raffle
ticket to carry our name;
the big package
to arrive, while
that little seed
we keep trying
to get unstuck
from our hearts
is all we
need.

Day 106

Luke 17:20

the kingdom comes
not with power,
but with those

who listen to
the meek;
not with loud shouts,
but with children
whispering hope in
each others' ears;
not with the cold
reality of death,
but with the
unexpected joy
of an empty grave.

Day 107

Luke 18:8

in the gardens,
where community
is planted alongside
vegetables;
in the playground
games,
where bullies
are transformed into
teammates;
in the businesses,
where compassion
takes priority over
profits,
may you find

faith.

Day 108

Luke 18:34

because
we let
resurrection joy
slip through our
hearts like
sand, even
after all this
time we
seem to understand
nothing
of what happened
on that morning, and
so
keep hope hidden
from
others.

Day 109

Deuteronomy 30:11

hope is as near
as a child
reaching for a
hand;
justice is as easy
as caring for
the most

vulnerable;
love is as nigh
as the butterfly
kiss
of a grandma;
grace is as simple
as a kind
word;
joy is as close
as splashing
in a
puddle.

Day 110

Psalm 48:9a

we study your
steadfast love, and
fail the test
when we mistreat others;
we dissect your
hope, leaving it
pinned to the tray,
while we turn out
the lights and leave;
we speed-read through
your grace, and
put it back
on the shelf to
gather dust.

Day 111

Luke 21:4

we give you
the change
left from our
frothy latte, and
think how much
we have sacrificed,
while
the barista
offers you her
heart,
and overflows
with
joy.

Day 112

Joshua 2:12c

may opening our
treasure be a
sign of generosity;
may our kind words
be a sign of
gentle grace;
may our embrace
be a sign
of genuine love;
may our lives

offered to others
be signs of
goodness where
so much is needed.

Day 113

Psalm 50:15

may we be
the family
for the lonely
who call on you;
the peace
in the war-torn
who cry out to you;
the grace
for all who
whisper their pain
to you.

Day 114

Luke 22:48

we betray you
not with a kiss,
but in the people
we kick to the side
of life;
not with a sword,
but with the sneer

we offer to
the hopeful;
not with a word,
but in the silence
uttered to
injustice.

Day 115

Luke 22:65

when we snigger
at those standing
on the corner
with handmade signs;
when we dump
neighbours into
a basket with
a toss-off remark;
when we whisper
about our friends
behind our hands,
while smiling at them,
we pile more
insults
on you.

Day 116

Proverbs 10:23a

in the evening,
we play
kick-the-con,
hide-and-seek
with the vulnerable,
freeze-tag
with refugees,
never noticing
how
we might offer
a hope,
an ear,
a job
instead.

Day 117

Luke 24:2, 5b

Hope strode out
of the grave, arms
wide open;
Joy turned cartwheels
as it sprang out of
the gloom;

Grace danced
out of the hollow, eager
to take us by the hand;
Life folded up
the grave clothes, longing
to wrap us in
laughter,
and
we keep trying to
stuff them back in
and roll the stone
shut.

Day 118

Luke 24:31

when i can
Hubbly see
the far shores
of the universe, but
not the jagged
edges of injustice;
when i can see
a microbe swim
in the sea, but
not the tear
on a child's cheek;
when i can
gaze at another
with lust, never
noticing their soul,

open my eyes
that i may recognise
you in
every person
every where
every moment.

Day 119

Psalm 53:4

eating bread containing grain
harvested by farmers
struggling to put food
on their tables;
piling on veggies
picked by
weary-backed
migrants;
adding a few
slices produced
by low-paid
meat-processors
and truck drivers, we
offer a quick
grace
as we bite
into the lives
of those we
rarely notice.

Day 120

John 1:38–39

in the morning,
we will find
you
standing by the
bed of the child
in the cancer unit;
in the afternoon,
we will find
you
rescuing immigrants
adrift on the sea
of indifference;
in the evening,
we will find
you
sleeping with the
homeless on the
streets,
if we only
go
and see.

Day 121

John 2:5

uh,
the part about
blessing kids,
and listening
to outsiders;
the reminders of
loving our enemies,
and doing good
every chance we have;
the hopes we would
throw parties
for the wasteful,
and give away
all that we have –

were we not listening?

Day 122

Psalm 55:2–3

the trolls just waiting
to bully;
the new post pinging
to interrupt my sleep;
the octothorpes

consuming my soul;
and Larry not
always bringing
happiness, so

why don't i
turn them off,
and rest
in you?

Day 123

Joshua 23:11

we carelessly
toss aside
those who
are in our way;
indifferent,
we do not
notice those
longing for hope;
too rushed,
we don't slow
down
to listen to
the songs of
children,
and then wonder
why you think
we don't love
you.

Day 124

John 4:4

when we
go through
shadows of grief,
may we reach hope;
as we travel
through rejection's pain,
may we see the
hearts waiting to welcome
us;
while we journey
through fear's famine,
may we smell
the aroma of
trust's feast;
may we tiptoe
through our parched
hearts,
to drink deeply
from love's well.

Day 125

Psalm 56:1a

in the silly songs
of preschoolers at
the storytime;
in the memories
of octogenarians
at a wedding;
in the dog
sticking its head
out the car window
and smiling;
in the moonbeam
teasing a kitten
at 3 in the morning,
your graciousness
pours out
upon us.

Day 126

John 4:46a

come again and
again, to
change our despair
into hope;
amend our legalism
into love;
transform our fear

into trust;
alter our apathy
into action;
revamp our
condemnation
into
compassion.

Day 127

Judges 6:7–8

the teacher
comforting
the bullied teenager;
the retiree
spending
a month each year
with disaster relief
groups;
the child
delivering food
parcels to rough sleepers:

your unnamed
prophets
are all around us
if we would only
listen.

Day 128

John 5:39

it is not in
the angry voices
that reach out
for our emptiness,
the social media
which promises
to be our family,
that life
which seems
to be just one purchase
away;
but it is
in
your heart
where we find
our deepest
longings.

Day 129

John 6:2

a casserole
placed in the
hands of a neighbour;
a call
to a legislator

advocating for
healthcare for all;
a drive
to the pharmacy
to pay for the prescription
of the homeless
fellow;
a journey
to accompany
our doctor
on a mission
to care for others,
may these
and so many more
be the signs
of what we
are doing for
the sick.

Day 130

John 6:25

when
we are wheeled
into surgery,
find a quiet corner
away from the bullies,
walk tearfully
to the graveside,
hesitantly enter

the interview room,
we find
you
already waiting
for us.

Day 131

Psalm 59:16

from songs composed
at sunrise,
to toe-tappers
in the gym;
from ditties
about your delight,
to lullabies of love,
i will sing
of your grace
until
it becomes an
earworm
in the world.

Day 132

John 7:15

you draw us
up
on your lap,
pulling out the
tattered set of
flash cards
you have carried
for years,
reminding us,
once again, that
G is for Grace
I is for Inclusion
J is for Justice
and on through
the alphabet of
life.

Day 133

John 8:7–8

those petulant
pebbles we
lodge in others' souls;
those rocks we
place so
those we detest
trip over

their narcissism;
those stones we
hurl
to crush the
hopes
of outsiders?

crumble them
into the canvas
on which you
finger-paint
'grace'

Day 134

John 8:29

when we
throw open
the door for
outsiders;
stand between
the kids
and their tormentors;
spend more
on the poor than
on ourselves,
we fill
you
with delight.

Day 135

Psalm 61:4

when the world
packs up
my life, setting
the suitcase out
on the porch (after
changing all
the locks
in the house), you
come along,
pick it up and,
taking me by
the hand,
lead me into
your heart.

Day 136

Ruth 2:14

put out extra
chairs at
the table;
cut the bread
into fairer
slices so all
may eat;
pour less wine

in the glasses,
so all will have
their thirst quenched;
hold hands
to grace the
food and fellowship:
welcome the
other into
your community.

Day 137

Ruth 3:1

may we be
the sanctuary
for all who
are chased
by their fears;
the home
for all who
have lost
everything;
the surety
for those
the world
distrusts.

Day 138

1 Samuel 2:8

in our rush
for more, we
shove others out
of the way, but
you pick them up
and dust them off;
we toss
the broken hopes
of friends in
the bin, but
you turn them
into treasures for your
heart;
we tell the servers
to stay in the kitchen
until the feast is over, but
you bring them out
and seat them at your
right hand.

Day 139

Psalm 64:1

as you listen,
hear my
hopes,
not just my hurts;
my
laughter,
not just my loneliness;
my
gratitude,
not just my grumbling;
my
faith,
not just my fears, and
save me
from the wearying
parts of
me!

Day 140

1 Samuel 7:12

the faded picture
of the mentor
who helped us find
the path through
life's brambles;
the marker in the garden
for the ashes

of the dog
who never left our side
during her best friend's
cancer;
the wearing down
of wedding rings
while the love
grows ever stronger:

Ebenezers
are all around us.

Day 141

John 12:26

'sure hope
someone
goes and helps
those poor folk
hit by the
flood/fire/storms/whatever,'
we tut before
turning to find
the funnies, while
you are already there
waiting
for your fellow
helpers
to get off
our comfy clichés
and join you.

Day 142

John 12:37

though
little children
welcome strangers
to their inner circles,
teenagers treat
the homeless
to meals,
parents work two
jobs to give
medicine to
loved ones,
seniors spend
'golden years' in
disaster relief,
still
we ask, 'where
can we see
hope
grace
joy
kindness?'

Day 143

Psalm 66:16

have you heard
about
those who ran
toward carnage;
those who
carried their friends
to safety;
those who refuse
to let fear control
their lives?

come, and listen ...

Day 144

Proverbs 12:28

may we sweep
aside the pebbles
of fear;
pull out the weeds
oppression planted;
fill in the potholes
caused by the
icy grip of despair,
so
all may walk
the way to
justice and hope.

Day 145

John 15:4a

because we are
sure
you won't let us
put our feet up
on the coffee table,
stand at the fridge
and drink milk right
from the container,
leave our dirty socks
scattered on the floor,
we
just aren't ready
to move into your heart,
or
have you move
into ours, if you
are going to spend
all your time
straightening up
everything.

Day 146

Psalm 68:6

you transform
your heart into
a boarding house

for the lonely;
you create
start-ups for
those just released
from jail;
you turn our
arid lives
into fountains
of hope.

Day 147

John 17:18

send us
not as experts
but as learners;
not as heroes
but as helpers;
not as professionals
but as migrant workers;
not as saviours,
but as servants;
not as ours,
but as theirs.

Day 148

John 18:8

facing evil
with love,
staring down injustice
with grace,
striding into death
for our sakes,
being at our side
through grief,

you are

so
we can be.

Day 149

1 Samuel 25:33

bless us
with common sense,
that we might
see others
through your eyes,
not our fears;
that we might
understand the loneliness
of those around us,

and not remain detached;
that we might
judge, not with
bitterness and anger,
but with compassion,
tipping the scales
towards grace.

Day 150

John 19:5

ecce homo
who would
be broken
to heal the world;
who would
walk into death's
cold embrace,
so our frozen hearts
might be thawed
in resurrection's love;
who would
give his life
so we might
find ours!

Day 151

John 20:5

we stare at
the empty
tomb afraid,
if we go in,
death
will leave us
lying there like
a pile of
empty clothes,
rather than believing
resurrection
will clothe us
in garments of grace.

Day 152

John 20:18

in the middle
of the muddle
of our messes,
may we see you
coming behind,
broom and pan
in hand, cleaning
up
after us, until

we start helping
others whose lives
are littered
behind them,
letting them in
on the secret of
faithfulness.

Day 153

John 21:17

when we think
the sheep
never stop
showing up,
always forget to
say 'thank you',
and that we
don't have enough
to share, remind us
that before you
ever challenged us
with this simple
task, you
fed us with
all we need.

Day 154

Psalm 69:13–14

when the world
dares me
to jump feet
first into fear's
quicksand, send
the Spirit with the
blueprints for
building a
bridge to your
hope.

Day 155

Acts 2:2–4

if we are not
willing to let
you take our breath
away, Spirit, and fill
us with your passion
for the broken,
the ignored,
the unloved,
the other, perhaps
we should just
replace the windows
of our hearts,

install a new sprinkler
system in our souls,
and keep mumbling
the same old, same old
we have done for
centuries.

Day 156

Acts 2:44–45

it is as simple
as bringing all
our accumulated
stuff for a yard
sale (letting folk
take all they can
put in a bag for $1
the last hour), and
using the funds
to feed the hungry,
offer shelter to the homeless
and a community to the
lonely ...

yet
it seems so
uncommon.

Day 157

Psalm 70:5a

when we would
hem and haw
with our reasons,
using our busyness,
our bum knees,
our bare cupboards
to put off caring,
double dare us
to beat you
in a sprint
to help the
vulnerable.

Day 158

Psalm 71:1a

may we become
a shelter
for those whose
grief keeps them awake,
a kitchen
for those who
hunger for hope,
a hospice
for those dying
of loneliness,
a panic room

for those bullied
by platitudes.

Day 159

Psalm 71:14

when i am
rocking furiously
on the porch,
in a grumble
over all that
has come my way,
take me by
the hand and sit me
beside you at
the scarred piano
teaching me hope's
chopsticks, so
we can play
as one.

Day 160

Psalm 71:18

despite the
stress highlights
dancing across
my thinning hair,
the canyons worry

has carved in
my visage,
the creaking
of my joints
with every move,
you cradle me
in your arms, whispering,
'my sweet baboo,
my beloved,
my joy.'

Day 161

Proverbs 14:20–21

as we deepen
in kindness
may we discover
the deep and
abiding
friendships
of those folk
others believe
are of no value
to themselves
or
anyone else.

Day 162

Psalm 72:2

in our marathon
to judge others,
based on our
worries,
doubts and
misconceptions,
may we be
refreshed with
the water of grace
you offer to us
as we race by, so
we can cross
the finish line
hand in hand
with those we
discover are
our sisters and brothers
in hope.

Day 163

Psalm 73:3

may our mentors be
the kids who
spend their lunch
money on fixings
for meals for

rough sleepers;
teenagers who
mow lawns and
babysit to
help pay for
a mate's chemo;
those whose humility
is simply who
they are, not
political expediency.

Day 164

Proverbs 14:31

so, it is actually
you
we think should
pull yourself up
by your bootstraps,
we mock for using
food stamps,
we call a
welfare cheat?!

Day 165

Acts 9:3

personally,
we hope our
conversion
is more
like a night light
keeping us from
stubbing our toes
in the shadows – not
a bright light
knocking us off
our ass-umptions.

Day 166

2 Samuel 24:24

may
our compassion
cost us our
apathy;
our love
cost us our
hate;
our hope
cost us our
bitterness ...

may every gift
we can offer
cost us our
desire to hoard.

Day 167

Acts 10:28

may those sticks
we use to
smack opponents
be used to build
shelter for the homeless;
may those stones
we use to
wall off outsiders
be used for a
bridge across anger's abyss;
may those words
of condemnation and ridicule
we hurl
at all who offend us
be turned into
love songs.

Day 168

Proverbs 15:4

when i
open my mouth
today, may
i plant seeds
of
hope,
wonder,
welcome,
grace.

Day 169

1 Kings 3:26

when leaders
(in their wisdom)
push to take
away all that
might give children
in poverty,
on the streets,
living in war zones,
a chance at life, will we
cry out
'have mercy'
or
'cut away'?

Day 170

Acts 13:41

we mock those
who
deliver meals
to the housebound,
tutor homeless
children,
advocate for
healthcare for
the most vulnerable,
defend the rights
of all people, never
noticing it is
you.

Day 171

Psalm 76:8a

you enunciated
judgement, but
it arrived in
the cry of a
baby born
into poverty, so
we might be
set free from
sin's injustice

and death's
onerous
stillness.

Day 172

Proverbs 15:11

we pile
all the brush, branches
and leaves we can
to cover over
the emptiness in
our hearts, but you
still jump
in feet first
to fill us with
you.

Day 173

Psalm 77:9

in our anger
towards others, we
forget about
grace,
trying to lock
its compassion,
hope,
joy

deep in the
recesses of our
hearts,
where
we have closeted
God.

Day 174

Psalm 79:10

when we expect
a whip, but
you hold a whiffle ball;
when we long
for a sword, only
to see you offering
a sandwich;
when we think
you should wield
an iron fist, but
are caressed by
a hand callused
from building shelters,
may we laugh
with joy, not
shed tears
of regret.

Day 175

Acts 16:9

the family members
we haven't spoken
to in years;
the residents of
the group home
down the street;
the transgender kids
in the schools
around us;
the opposition party
folk living
next door;
the immigrants
in line with us
at the stores:
so many
Macedonias,
so little time,
so much resistance
to crossing
over.

Day 176

Proverbs 15:25

early each morning,
you drive down
the street, stopping
and tossing the scraps
from our overbuilt lives
in the back of
your rusty pickup,
taking them with you
as you join the Carpenter
in rebuilding the hope
of the forgotten.

Day 177

Psalm 78:16

strike our
hard-as-flint
hearts, so
grace may flow
into the deserts
burnished by cynicism;
transform the
bitterness pooling
in our souls
into streams
of hope flowing
to the sea.

Day 178

1 Kings 19:11–12

in the utter quiet
of a candle flickering
on a winter's night;
in the gentle rocking
of a cradle
in a nursery;
in the winds
of justice breaking
oppression
into dust, you
pass by
us
so we can
notice and
follow.

Day 179

Acts 18:9

we have all sorts
of opinions
we proclaim loudly –
about the weather,
politics, sports,
and religion, but
when it comes to
poverty,

prejudice,
inclusion,
injustice
we suddenly develop
laryngitis.

Day 180

1 Kings 22:14

may
we not turn
your passion
for peace into
platitudes,
your compassion
for the vulnerable into
clichés,
your grace into
generalities,
your justice into
fables.

Day 181

Acts 20:32a

when the twitter
bombs continue
to fall,
when anger's waves

crash on our
souls' shores,
when bitterness
is offered as
a balm to our hearts,
cradle us with
grace
and draw us closer
to you.

Day 182

Psalm 78:72

when they show
up at our doors,
in duffle coat,
old hat and with
battered suitcase
in hand, may
we not overlook
the tag reading,
'please take care
of this child of mine,
thank you' as
we welcome them
into our hearts,
as you did us.

Day 183

2 Kings 5:13

we find rocket science
higher math
or
textual criticism
a piece of cake
compared to
feeding the hungry
welcoming the stranger
adopting the forgotten,
the living in peace
we are asked
to do.

Day 184

Proverbs 16:9

we reprogramme our
soul's GPS so
we can do what we want
go where we will
be who we idolise, then
you
take us by the
hand
to lead us
(barefoot)
to baptism's beach

where we will
surf on grace's waves
until falling asleep
exhausted.

Day 185

Psalm 80:5

you flavour
the bread of
life with
the tang
of your tears,
and transform
your bitter
grief
into
grace's cup.

Day 186

Acts 24:15a

i cling tight
to the hope
that
the most vulnerable
will be valued more,
the hungry will
be offered banquets,

foreclosed properties will
be shared with the homeless,
the lonely will
be welcomed like family and,
in God,
i open
my hands to
share.

Day 187

Psalm 81:5b–6

in the soft breath
of a baby
against our cheek;
in the silly jokes
of 9-year-olds;
in the infuriating
questions of
teenagers,
our fears
our worries
our doubts
are taken away.

Day 188

Proverbs 16:22a

may
i drink deeply
of your Spirit
before i
speak to
(or about)
another.

Day 189

Psalm 81:16

you lay out
a picnic
of Grace's sandwiches,
Hope's strawberry/rhubarb pies,
Wonder's potato salad and
the finest vintage Peace-makes,
but
we
would rather gnaw
on our bitter
hearts and
chug-a-lug
anger's acid.

Day 190

Psalm 82:3–4

shelter for those
caught in life's storms;
food for children
hungering for hope;
a welcome to all
pushed aside by the world;
standing nose to nose
with oppression's supporters;
calling the vulnerable
our sisters and brothers ...
... these are some of the ways
we can pull God's beloved
out of those fists tight with

judgement.

Day 191

Psalm 83:1

at the corner
of Discord
and Distrust, where
we rant and rail,
trying to kick the
soapboxes out
from under those

we don't want to speak,
you pull up
in your food truck,
setting up tables
and offering tea
and scones, encouraging
us to close our mouths
and open our hearts.

Day 192

Proverbs 16:28

slipping into
the restaurant booth
while our best friend
is on a call outside,
Tattle begins
to bandy on about
what they are (really!)
saying
about us, hoping
to split the dessert
with us when we
get into a huff.

Day 193

Psalm 84:2a

i yearn for
your justice,
where the oppressed
are set free;
your house, where
you make popcorn balls
for snacks;
your yard, where
we can chase fireflies
until the stars
come out
to watch over us
as we snuggle in
our sleeping bags.

Day 194

Psalm 84:10

this day,
may i
serve meals
to the hungry,
run through
sprinklers with kids,
stand in the rain
with all who
have had the doors

of hope slammed
in their faces.

Day 195

Romans 2:4

not
judgement
punishment
forever abandonment, but
gentleness
acceptance
tolerance
are the treasures
God
has in store for us.

Day 196

Proverbs 17:9

like that pebble
in a shoe, a
grudge rubs a
blister on our
soul, but
your grace removes
it, so
we can walk
in hope with
the one who hurt us.

Day 197

Psalm 85:13

Justice & Daughters Restoration
leads the way, filling
in oppression's potholes
with grace and hope, as
God
takes the vulnerable
by the hand
to lead them
home.

Day 198

Amos 5:24

forgive us
when we
think justice is
best served a
drop at a time, and
we dam up hope's
river with our
forms and regulations.

Day 199

Romans 5:1–2

we've triple-firewalled
and 64-bit-encrypted our
hearts, but
you simply type
JESUS
in as the password
and hack us, so
we can be infected
with the grace virus.

Day 200

Amos 8:4

in our rush
to get the newest
of the in-est
of the faddest,
we knock over
those who
can't even afford
the leftovers
we so casually toss
aside

in our rush ...

Day 201

Hosea 2:15a

we stand,
staring despondently
through
the links in
the fence, then
you come along,
picking the lock,
patching the pitfalls,
opening the concession stand,
and
letting us in
to play on the fields
of wonder.

Day 202

Psalm 88:3

Fret, Sweat and
their brother, Bother,
keep nudging me
closer to the edge, whispering,
'it's just a short
step down,'
but
you are there

building a bridge
so we can
cross the Pit
hand in hand.

Day 203

Romans 7:15

i know i
should be
gracious,
forgiving,
accepting, but
as a lifelong
member
of the Saved
Beyond a Doubt
(reformed) Church,
i am guided
by that strong
streak of
self-justification
to control those
around me.

Day 204

Romans 8:1

not yesterday,
where we spend
so much time
kicking our mistakes
around and around;
not tomorrow,
which we hope
doesn't come, with
its chances to
screw up again, but
this day
this moment
this breath
there is hope
forgiveness
acceptance

now.

Day 205

Hosea 11:8

like the mother
helping her son mix
another cake after
the third try burnt;

like the daughter
calmly working with
her refugee father
to learn a new language;
like the 6-year-old
patiently, and painstakingly,
practising writing letters
over and over and over,
you never give up on us –
you
never
give up!

Day 206

Romans 8:38–39

not yesterday,
which moulds in the
garbage under the sink;
or tomorrow,
which hangs in
the closet waiting
to be put on;
not politicians
who could care less
about anyone but themselves;
or celebrities
who will be who
others want them to be
for a price;

not weary, ageing bodies;
not foolishness who
sticks out a foot to trip us;
not our pride, which
grows larger with
every lie we tell ourselves;

nothing
can keep us apart
from God
because of
everything Jesus
did for us.

Day 207

Psalm 89:14

on the front porch,
you sit in the
rocker carved from
the tree of justice, ready
to dry us off
and pull us up
on your lap when
we are done playing
with Hesed and
Joy in the sprinklers.

Day 208

Romans 10:8

each year, we
get the booster
immunising us
against your word, because,
if we catch it,
we might become
contagious
and infect others
with
grace
peace
mercy
hope
joy.

Day 209

Psalm 89:28

here's the deal:

not just
when we are
good,
or in church,
or praying,
or caring, but
forever …

unconditional
unshakeable
unrelenting …

love.

Day 210

Romans 12:18

perhaps
if we listened to
you
more than
twittering politicians,
foul-mouthed communicators,
even grudging inner voices, we
might discover how
to live with others
in love, hope, grace

perhaps.

Day 211

Romans 13:10

help us
to have the
good sense
to come in
out of the

twitterstorm,
and feed the hungry,
read to little kids,
listen to the stories
of grandparents,
build hope out of fears.

Day 212

Romans 14:17

the kingdom
is not
most-visited websites,
multi-campus churches,
higher television ratings,
but
justice for the most vulnerable,
reconciled communities,
learning new dance steps from the Spirit,
being,
not just talking.

Day 213

Romans 15:13

may we go
tubing with
Laughter and Grace
down the rippling
waters of hope,
climbing out on
the banks at the
end of the day to
share the feast
grilled out by
Spirit

all day long.

Day 214

Psalm 90:1

you were
the yard where
we could lie
on our backs
and see animals
in clouds;
you are
the shelter
we return to
at the end
of weary days

to rest safe
in your peace;
you will be
the retirement home
where we can
spend the rest
of our days in
hope and grace.

Day 215

Psalm 90:14

in a knot,
we tumble down
the stairs, rubbing
sleep from our
eyes, finding
you
at the table, where
we are served bowls
of Grace Crispies
sprinkled with *hesed*,
swimming in milk and honey,
and
after wiping our mouths
and giving you a kiss,
we rush out
to play in your
wonder.

Day 216

1 Corinthians 1:4–5

by your
grace, i
can see the
broken hearts others
hide behind, a
wall bricked with
bravado, and
so whisper the
hope (not
the hurt),
the forgiveness (not
the foolishness),
the love (not
the loathing),
they need.

Day 217

1 Corinthians 1:25

when we would
put on fancy robes with
doctoral bars,
preaching tabs and
beautiful stoles, you
dress us
in the rainbow wig,

red nose,
floppy shoes,
polka-dot pants
and starry-spangled shirt,
saying,
'now, go be
the good news.'

Day 218

1 Corinthians 2:10

putting on her
work boots and
strapping on the
headlamp, the Spirit
continues to mine
your heart each day
for
the grace,
hope,
peace,
wonder and
other resources
which fuel our faith.

Day 219

Psalm 92:1–3

from that
snap, crackle and
pop of wonder at
breakfast,
to the mid-morning
cuppa break and
scone slathered with
grace,
to the late-night
warm glass of peace
before we drift off to
sleep,
sing us your
songs of hope and love
in every moment.

Day 220

1 Corinthians 4:1

we could take
the gospel and,
by giving it
so many plot twists,
characters who
appear only once,
clues that disappear

down rabbit holes
never to be seen again,
manage to
confuse everyone;

or
we could just
reveal from the
start that it was
you
in our hearts
with grace
who did it

(the butler who killed death).

Day 221

Psalm 93:4

rather than
continue to
drive our lives
into the flash floods
of fear and fury,
let us float
on that still pool
of your heart.

Day 222

Psalm 94:9

we sit on the park bench,
holding hands with
loneliness, as the world
rushes by oblivious, until
you come by
on your tandem bike, asking,
'want to go on an
adventure?'

Day 223

Psalm 94:18

(while the world
waits around the
corner, ready to
laugh its head off at me),
you rush up
and catch me, as
i step on
the peel tossed
on the sidewalk
by foolishness, and
begin to topple
down.

Day 224

Proverbs 19:27

you stand at
the board, showing
how grace
hope
justice
might work
in our lives, as
we slip out
the door, following
the pied piper of
foolishness.

Day 225

Psalm 95:7b

over the bile
of the radio bullies,
may we hear hope;
turning down the rhetoric
of bellicose politicians,
may we hear peace;
refusing to listen
to anger's enticing ads,
may we hear love,
and then speak
with our lives.

Day 226

Psalm 96:10

you slowly,
patiently,
craft your hopes,
one heart,
one person,
one community
at a time,
the measuring tape
of fairness
always in your hand.

Day 227

Psalm 97:6

if we took
out the earbuds,
we might hear
the frogs' chorus;
if we looked
up from our devices,
we might see
justice offering hope;
if we stopped
worrying about how
many folk are clinging
to every social media

post we make,
we might just
find you with those
we have failed to notice;

if

Day 228

1 Corinthians 10:24

when i
long to be
top dog,
hand me a
shovel to help
you
clean the shelter's
kennels.

Day 229

1 Corinthians 11:31

in my courtroom,
i am always
acquitted, but
others should bring
a good defence
attorney!

Day 230

Song of Songs 2:8

in the laughter
of children playing
leapfrog;
in the mother
patiently teaching
her son how
to change a flat tyre;
in the octogenarian
softly whispering
love songs to
his partner,

we hear your voice,
Beloved.

Day 231

1 Corinthians 13:4–8a

love
listens to grandpa's story
for the umpteenth time
(without rolling its eyes);
kisses every
dirty boo-boo;
does not laugh
behind another's back;
stands between

the vulnerable
and the bullies;

love
carries the broken hearts of others,
sees good in each person,
cares when everyone else doesn't,
knows evil eclipses good but for a moment;
love always is
love.

Day 232

1 Corinthians 14:9

may our words
of hope
grace
justice
be clear and concise,
lest
they blow away
like dandelion puffs.

Day 233

1 Corinthians 14:20

rather than
giving hate and
evil
to others as

hand-me-downs, let
us put them out
by the curb,
to be recycled into
hope and
grace.

Day 234

Psalm 102:1

whether hurled
like thunderbolts
or whispered in
hope, you
gather our prayers
to your heart, where
they are melted
into healing balm
for our lives.

Day 235

1 Corinthians 15:1

sucking on bitterness,
it is hard to preach
good news;
hands full of anger,
it is hard to share
the gospel.

Day 236

Proverbs 20:27

though we try
to burn the
bulb out, you
continue to
shine in our
souls so we
can find the way
to you.

Day 237

1 Corinthians 16:6

we can find
a resort that
provides every amenity
we long for, at
a 'special' price, or
we can rest
in your heart
on our pilgrimage
to grace,

perhaps.

Day 238

2 Corinthians 1:4

because
we have been
rescued
cradled
restored,
we must …

Day 239

Psalm 103:14

dusting off your
hands, you
breathe a sigh
of grace,
sending
us to be
your hope,
your joy,
your welcome.

Day 240

2 Corinthians 2:5a,8

forgiveness
is not a quick
fix

but the long,
slow
restoration of
two hearts.

Day 241

2 Corinthians 2:15

like warm
bread just
out of the oven,
may we be the
bouquet
of grace
for those
hungering for
hope.

Day 242

2 Corinthians 3:12

may our
hope
be bolder
than our
flagrant
fears.

Day 243

Micah 4:4

in your mercy,

guns into guitars,
missiles into food silos,
violence into vineyards,
anger into acceptance;

please

Day 244

Micah 6:3

let us not
weary you
with our
whining, but
energise you
with our
empathy.

Day 245

2 Corinthians 5:20b

when God
moved
toward us

in Christ, it
was not to checkmate
us, but
to swaddle us
in grace.

Day 246

2 Corinthians 6:12

let love
not be a
grudge lodged
deep in our souls,
but joy offered
without question
to others.

Day 247

2 Corinthians 7:2a

let us take
down the
'No vacancy'
sign in our hearts,
so we may welcome
your terrifying
compassion.

Day 248

Isaiah 8:17

though
i cannot see you
through the fog
of my foolishness,
i will wait, hoping
you know the
way to me.

Day 249

Isaiah 11:11a

leftovers of love
will feed
multitudes;
odds and ends
of hope
will weave justice;
a ribbon
of grace
will bind
us into one

on that day.

Day 250

Isaiah 14:30a

let us welcome
dreamers to
our feast, and
tuck the
worn out into
bed,
while others
twitter their
thumbs.

Day 251

2 Corinthians 10:7a

patience
in the dog
waiting for the
kids to come home;
love
in the hands
held in a hospice;
hope
in the child
searching for a
friend;

do we notice?

Day 252

2 Corinthians 11:1

sometimes
a pie in the
face
is worth
more than all
those pious masks
we think we
must wear.

Day 253

Isaiah 25:4

in meals
handed out to
rough sleepers;
in neighbours
taking fresh-baked bread
to the newcomers,

you are
as you always
have been.

Day 254

Isaiah 27:5

when we would play
on the floor, using
our grudges
as jacks, may
we climb up
in your lap, letting
your heartbeat
cradle us in
peace.

Day 255

Psalm 107:9

with grace,
you quench
those parched
by fear;
with justice,
you feed all
weakened by
oppression's
starvation rations.

Day 256

Proverbs 22:24

outrage
is more
contagious
than any flu;
bitter words
flung at others
do more damage
than a weapon.

Day 257

Isaiah 35:8a

the folk
in waders
and boats
searching from
house to house;
the line crews
on 16-hour
shifts;
the nun
clearing debris
after a storm, all
know the
Holy Way.

Day 258

Galatians 2:10

if only
we
thought of
those who
have nothing,
as often as
we long for
everything.

Day 259

Isaiah 40:2c

we expect
a right hook
followed by
a mean uppercut,
but you hand
us a plate of
warm grace-chip
cookies and
a cold glass of hope.

Day 260

Galatians 3:24

while
the babysitter
is recording
all our errors,
you sneak us
into the backyard
to play in
grace's sprinkler.

Day 261

Isaiah 43:19a

so fixed
on rebuilding
yesterday, we
cannot see
the tomorrow
you are
imagining
(for us).

Day 262

Isaiah 45:19

not in the
whispered seductions
of fear;

not in the early-morning
tweetstorms;
not in the category 5
chaos of hate;

but
in the silent
watching of a
parent over
a child;
in the justice
which sweeps out
oppression;
in the words
of welcome
offered to
outsiders

we will find
you

Day 263

Psalm 109:1

whisper your
love and
grace
until their echoes
drown out
the silence of
my fears.

Day 264

Galatians 6:9a

just when
we cannot
lift another
finger, you
pour us
a cuppa
grace,

just so we can …

Day 265

Isaiah 52:8b

in
the touch of a nurse,
the kindness of a teacher,
the grace of kids,
the wisdom of teenagers,
the hopes of the outcast,
the forgiveness of the hurt,
we find you
hiding in plain sight.

Day 266

Isaiah 55:6

no need to
shout …
God is as
close
as our
next breath.

Day 267

Isaiah 58:9b–10

in your community
of neighbours, no one
hungers,
huddles in loneliness,
holds grudges,
hates,
fears,
hurts another.

Day 268

Isaiah 61:1a

to
plant hope in
despair's field;
offer grace to
fear's hungry hordes;
swaddle the
broken with tenderness.

Day 269

Psalm 112:9a

not hoarders,
but helpers;
not hoops to jump
through,
but hope;
not reluctantly,
but joyfully;

this is our calling.

Day 270

Isaiah 65:24

may
we be the
hope-hand-help
others are seeking;
may
we be the
ear-heart-love
for the forgotten.

Day 271

Nahum 1:15a

the boots of
anger
are so comfy, yet
we find
the soft bunny
slippers of peace
too tight a fit.

Day 272

Zephaniah 2:3b

let us
persist in
finding justice;
let us
become as
simple as kids
who bear
no grudges.

Day 273

Philippians 1:27a

peace, not petulance,
hope, not hoops,
joy, not jousting,
grace, not grumpiness,
love, not loneliness,
only.

Day 274

Jeremiah 3:4

you
sit at the
corner table, ready
to catch up

with us over
coffee, whenever
we are ready.

Day 275

Jeremiah 5:1b

even if
it is only
two folk
linking arms,
injustice knows
that it has
met its match.

Day 276

Jeremiah 6:16

when we stand
at the intersection
of Peace and
Hope,
why
do we rush
to get tangled
in the

brambles?

Day 277

Psalm 116:12

i will
dig wells
for thirsty villages,
plant gardens
for food pantries,
break bread
with those i
can't abide.

Day 278

Jeremiah 11:13a

like a hundred
paper cuts,
my gods
bleed out
my
soul.

Day 279

Colossians 2:15

you
downsized death,
assigning it to
resurrection's mailroom.

Day 280

Jeremiah 15:16a

when I had
lost everything
but your
words,
i had
all
i needed.

Day 281

Colossians 4:2

may prayer
open
our eyes
to the unnoticed,
our ears
to the ignored,
our hearts
to the disfavoured,
our souls
to you.

Day 282

Jeremiah 18:4b

reshape me
from that
dusty piece on
my ego's mantel
into
that wide-mouthed
jar
where others
can pour their
brokenness.

Day 283

Jeremiah 23:5a

mornings
as grace
rises over the horizon;
midday
lunches for
hungry seniors;
peace-filled
afternoons in
war zones;
evenings
where hope cradles
the oppressed;

come,
days of the Lord –
come!

Day 284

1 Thessalonians 4:18

when
peace prods
the indifferent,
hope stirs
the oppressed,
laughter enlivens
hospital rooms,
wonder brightens
a bored kid,

words
are no longer
just
alphabet soup.

Day 285

1 Thessalonians 5:19

we stop, drop and
roll
the Spirit
every chance
we get, but
you
keep igniting
her wildfire of
grace.

Day 286

Jeremiah 29:14a

every time we say,
'let's play hide-and-seek'
and start to
count to 100
with our souls closed,
you stand
in the middle
of life (holding
a big arrow
pointing down
at you).

Day 287

Jeremiah 30:10a

there is
nothing
under the
bed,
hiding in the
corner,
tapping on the
window,
tiptoeing behind
us that
you
can't handle.

Day 288

Psalm 119:42

when the bullies
corner us,
demanding
'cough it up!' may
we whisper
gently,
'hesed'.

Day 289

Jeremiah 31:15a

in
#metoo,
memories sifted
from ashes,
communities
recovering from
too many storms
to name,
we find our
way to
Ramah.

Day 290

Psalm 119:49

however
often
i forget, you
evoke grace
for me
in every moment.

Day 291

Psalm 119:60

may i leave
my tortoise
shell behind
as i seek
to love you
and those around me.

Day 292

Proverbs 25:20

you offer
your own heart
for our grief
to nibble on, so
ours
can be balmed
by your
grace.

Day 293

Jeremiah 44:4a

in the young boy
offering half his sandwich
to the rough sleeper;
in the adolescent
standing between the bully
and the socially awkward;
in the parent
who helps kids with homework
before heading to job #2;
in the grandparent
who builds little free libraries
in the neighbourhoods,
we find your
persistent
prophets
among us.

Day 294

1 Timothy 6:8

give me
silence
a cuppa
a warm scone
a good book
a loved, well-worn shirt, and
ah ...

Day 295

2 Timothy 1:5

Gramp's wisdom,
Mum's patience,
Auntie's humour,
Sis's love,
Little bro's hope
are all spliced
into my faith
DNA.

Day 296

2 Timothy 2:9c

every time we
try to crate-train
grace, you
sneak in and
set it free
to run wild
in the world.

Day 297

Psalm 119:94a

every time
i end up
where i shouldn't
be, you
find me, and
lead me back
home.

Day 298

2 Timothy 4:2b

there is never a
right day
week
month
year
to confront
injustice, just
every moment.

Day 299

Psalm 119:109a

when my
life slips
through my
fingers, you
pick it up
and hand it
back to me
before the
robotic Hoover
sweeps it up.

Day 300

Proverbs 26:4a

in a flood
of tweets,
build an
ark
out of
compassion and
truth.

Day 301

Lamentations 1:21a

we could
cradle others,
drying their tears
with our hope,

but

Day 302

Lamentations 3:21

your hope
is that
earworm
i cannot
get out of
my soul –

thankfully!

Day 303

Lamentations 3:57

when fear
comes
trick or treating
in our lives, you

hand us a piece of
hope
to drop in
their pillowcase,
and we go back
to making hot cocoa.

Day 304

Obadiah 12a

rather than
turning out
the porch light, may
we pour grace
into the basket
held out by
the one whose
scream
is not a mask.

Day 305

Joel 2:17c

where?
sheltering kids
taken off a
crumpled school bus;
responding to
the injured

and dying;
parading with
neighbours
into fear's
shadows ...

there
God.

Day 306

Joel 3:18b

let us join
all souls
in drifting down
your stream
of grace
to the picnic
which awaits.

Day 307

Hebrews 4:16a

we'd be quicker
to approach
the throne of
grace, if
it were a
rocking chair
where we

could climb up
into your lap.

Day 308

Hebrews 5:11a

while
we think it's
quantum physics, faith
is simply a
bee,
where
every word
is spelled

g-r-a-c-e.

Day 309

Hebrews 6:18

when you
hand hope
off to us,
let us wrap
our souls and
hearts
around it
so we do not
fumble.

Day 310

Psalm 119:168

no matter
how much
the world's
GPS tries
to recalculate
our lives, you
show us the
way.

Day 311

Ezekiel 14:3a

we take in
idols
like they are
stray cats, so
is it any surprise
we have no
room for
God
in our hearts?

Day 312

Proverbs 27:9b

the gentle grace
of those
who love us
despite our
worst selves
brings
healing to
our souls.

Day 313

Psalm 121:4

no matter
how many times
we awake
in the night
hours of life, we
find you
sitting by the
bed,
ready to
hand us a
glass of water,
wipe our
runny souls,
read us a
story until we
drift back to sleep.

Day 314

Psalm 122:2

on the playground
with little kids,
by the bed
in a hospice,
working in a
shelter,
packing boxes
at a food pantry,
we
are on
holy ground.

Day 315

Psalm 123:2a

in the finger
tracing words
on a page;
in the tiny hand
reaching up
to take ours;
in the arm
of support for
a teetering partner;
in the open palm
of welcome

to a stranger, we
recognise you.

Day 316

Proverbs 27:20a

no matter
how often we feed
the Destroyer of
our hopes and dreams,
there
is always
a hunger
in the pit
of its
stomach.

Day 317

Psalm 124:7a

while the Fouler
was busy partying,
you
crept in
and, opening
death's cage,
set us
free.

Day 318

Psalm 125:2

as our nightmares
tiptoe down
the hallway, creaking
every fear-board
with each step,
you swaddle us
in grace,
drawing us up
into your lap,
whispering hope
in our hearts.

Day 319

Hebrews 12:15a

we are not
to hoard
grace
as if it were
a scarce
commodity, but to
pour it into
others' lives
as if it were
a bottomless
cup of
coffee.

Day 320

Hebrews 13:8

yesterday
you were cradling
children in a school
lockdown;
this morning
you are standing
with the workers
on the corner hoping
for a day job;
tomorrow and tomorrow and tomorrow
you will be
wherever we are,
even when we
don't notice.

Day 321

James 1:22

strangely,
peace
hope
grace
mercy
never seem
to end up
on our
to-do lists.

Day 322

James 2:6a

sadly, we
treat those who
struggle to put
food on the table,
cannot seem to
hold a job,
stand on street corners
holding handmade signs,
as if
they were
dishonourably discharged
from life.

Day 323

James 3:6a

sometimes
those remarks
we think are so
scintillating, reduce
the souls
of others
to cinders.

Day 324

James 4:11a

too often,
our dictionaries
seem to have
words
relating to
compassion
hope
grace
acceptance
removed by
our carping
hearts.

Day 325

Psalm 130:3

that ruler
you could
use to smack
our hands, you
take to measure
our growth in
grace.

Day 326

Psalm 131:2a

help me
to give my
soul
a timeout
whenever
it throws a
tantrum,
wanting its
own way,
not yours.

Day 327

1 Peter 2:17a

the rough sleeper
you would step over,
lift up;
the worker
you would bully,
befriend;
the vulnerable
you would mock,
laud;
the hungry
you would drive past,
welcome to your table;
the door of your heart
you would slam shut to everyone,
take off its hinges.

Day 328

1 Peter 3:15b

may we not
dam
up that hope,
but let it
overflow our
souls, so
others might
swim in its
delight.

Day 329

1 Peter 4:9

may we
feed the hungry
without worrying if
we will get dessert;
offer the homeless
our guest room
without hiding
the valuables;
listen to the
heartbroken
without mentioning
our creaky knees.

Day 330

Psalm 135:1a,2a

in the gym,
with the little kids;
in the shelter,
making up
the beds;
in the hospice,
holding a hand;
in the silence,
bathed in your
grace,
we are at home –
and sing.

Day 331

2 Peter 1:9a

when we look at
others
through the thick and
fear-spotted lenses
of judgement, polish
our souls with
grace and compassion
so we can see them
with our
hearts.

Day 332

Proverbs 29:7

now,
let us close
the books and turn
our knowledge into
jobs
hope
homes
grace
life
for the most
vulnerable
around us.

Day 333

2 Peter 3:10a

while we sleep,
you tiptoe in,
gathering up
all our foolish
frailties, taking
them back to
your workshop, where
you transform them
into gifts of grace,
returning them
before we
awake.

Day 334

1 John 2:28a

scanning the
columns for places
in the low-rent
areas of life, we
never notice
your full-page ad
about your heart
which has more
than enough room for
everyone.

Day 335

Psalm 136:23

when we
stumble and
fall into misery, you
jump in
to show us
the way out.

Day 336

1 John 3:2b

in the worker
doing a double shift
for the expectant dad;

in the child
collecting toys
not intended
for her;
in the older couple
taking in a
homeless family,
we
find you.

Day 337

Psalm 137:1

we could sit by
and simply add
our tears
to the rivers
of injustice, or
remember God's
hope
and use it
to build bridges
leading to new life.

Day 338

Psalm 138:3a

an involuntary gasp
at a super-moon;
a choke of rage
at injustice;

a muffled laugh
at my own foolishness;
a peal of joy
while dancing in the snow:

you hear
and store it all
in your heart.

Day 339

Psalm 139:5

just
as i am about
to shatter
into a million
pieces, you
cradle me in
your hands, filling
all the cracks
with the glue
of grace.

Day 340

2 John:6a

… and

dragging a tree
through the snow

toward a waiting
knot of kids;
singing
in the rain
with our furry
friends;
massaging the
weary feet
of our beloved
at the end of a long day,

this is love.

Day 341

Zechariah 1:13

we hurl insults:
you offer praise;
we fling profanities:
you whisper grace;
our words pull
the rug out from
others: you
envelop folk with
hope and
love.

Day 342

Zechariah 8:12a

you give each
one of us
a small packet
of seeds so, if
we dare plant them,
a field of peace
will spring up
from one edge
of creation
to the other.

Day 343

Psalm 140:5

but you
clothe me in
bands of compassion;
lower a ladder
to the bottom
of the pit;
clear my way
of stumbles,
all out of
love.

Day 344

Zechariah 12:10a

we could continue
to dunk people
in deep pools
of bitterness, or
bathe them in
compassion,
drying them
off with our
prayers of hope.

Day 345

Psalm 140:12

when it comes
to caring for
the most vulnerable,
our minds are
with you, but
our hearts,
mouths,
hands?

Day 346

Psalm 141:1

when i drag
my feet, each
step more reluctant
than the one before, you
run to pick me up,
twirling me around
and around,
whispering sweet everythings
to ears stopped
up
with the cotton candy
of platitudes.

Day 347

Psalm 142:2

your desk is
piled high with file
after file
of grumbles, as you
try to clear them, yet
when we knock
on the door asking
if you have a
minute,
you push them aside,
'of course – I

have all the time
you need.'

Day 348

Revelation 5:6

not a warrior,
but a peacemaker;
not a grudge-holder,
but a grace-sharer;
not a bully,
but a baby;
not a lion,
but the Lamb.

Day 349

Malachi 1:1

sometimes,
your words are
boulders that stoop
my heart to
the ground, but
then, they are
feathers that
tickle my
soul
with delight.

Day 350

Revelation 7:17c

by your grace,
our tears
are transformed
into cups of
grace, offered
to all parched
by loneliness,
loss,
despair.

Day 351

Revelation 8:1

perhaps, in
the silence
of Advent, we
can hear the
heartbeats of
children, and the
hopebeats
of their
parents.

Day 352

Ezra 3:13

whether
shouts of joy
echoing down
hospital hallways, or
overwhelming grief
flowing down the
streets of injustice,
may we listen ...

Day 353

Psalm 145:6b

replacing
the politicos'
empty words with
cries for justice;
building bridges to
others, not walls
between us;
seeing the poor
as holy families
to serve, we
declare your
greatness.

Day 354

Psalm 145:13b

compassion,
not confrontation;
grace,
not grudges;
wide-open arms,
not exclusion,
all
for us.

Day 355

Psalm 145:16

everything we
need is found
in the palm
of
your hands,
where you have
engraved our
hearts, to always
hold us in every
moment.

Day 356

Proverbs 31:8

may we be
the voice for
those ignored;
the love for
everyone rejected;
the healing for
the world's broken;
the heart for
all who are
orphaned by hate.

Day 357

Psalm 146:9

may we not only
notice
the stranger
the bullied child
the trembling grandparent
the lone-weary worker
but
see them as
your beloved
children.

Day 358

Revelation 16:17

in the silence
in the night
in the whispers
of the angels
in the questions
of the shepherds
the very air grows
still,
as a baby
takes its first
breath, sighing,
'it is done!'

Day 359

Psalm 147:15

early in the morning,
your word
tiptoed into
our lives,
swaddled in our
hopes and
mangered in your
love.

Day 360

Proverbs 31:20

when the most
vulnerable
reach out with
their emptiness, may
we not recoil
in disgust,
but
open our hands
hearts
blessings
to fill them.

Day 361

Revelation 19:9a

no matter who
we are,
how many times
we dine at
temptation's table,
there is a setting
and a card with our
name
at the wedding
party
at the end of
time.

Day 362

Psalm 148:7

seahorses and
humpbacks,
crawling toddlers
and yawning teens,
knee-creaking
seniors and
snap-fingered
singers,
squirrels running
faster than
barking dogs –
all praise you!

Day 363

Revelation 20:12b

by your grace,
every name
(including mine)
is written in
your book
of life in
permanent ink.

Day 364

Revelation 21:25

leaving the door
wide open, you
sit at the table, our
pictures bathed
in the warmth
of the Spirit
lamp,
waiting
for us to come
home.

Day 365

Revelation 22:21

you begin by
crafting grace
out of chaos;
grace is
the best friend
who never abandons
us;
grace will walk
us home to
you.

Day 366 (For a leap year)

Mark 10:15

give us one more day
to discover we are your children:
welcoming the new kids
into our games and chats,
drawing imaginary creatures
with chalk on sidewalks,
splashing through puddles
after a rainstorm,
offering you a cup of tea
and biscuits on the porch,
falling asleep on the gentle grass
in the shade of the tree of life.